First American Edition published in 2010 by
Enchanted Lion Books
20 Jay Street, Studio M-18,
Brooklyn, NY 11201
Originally published in French as *Gandhi*
© 2007 Bayard Éditions Jeunesse
Translated by Robert Brent
All rights reserved in accordance with the provisions
of the Copyright Act 0f 1956 as amended.
A CIP record is on file with the Library of Congress
ISBN: 978-1-59270-094-3
Printed in July 2010 in China by South China Printing Co. Ltd., King Yip
(Dong Guan) Printing & Packaging Factory Co. Ltd., Daning Administrative District,
Humen Town, Dong Guan City, Guangdong Province 523930

Gandhi

His Life, His Struggles, His Words

Written by Élisabeth de Lambilly

Illustrated by Séverine Cordier

ENCHANTED LION BOOKS

NEW YORK

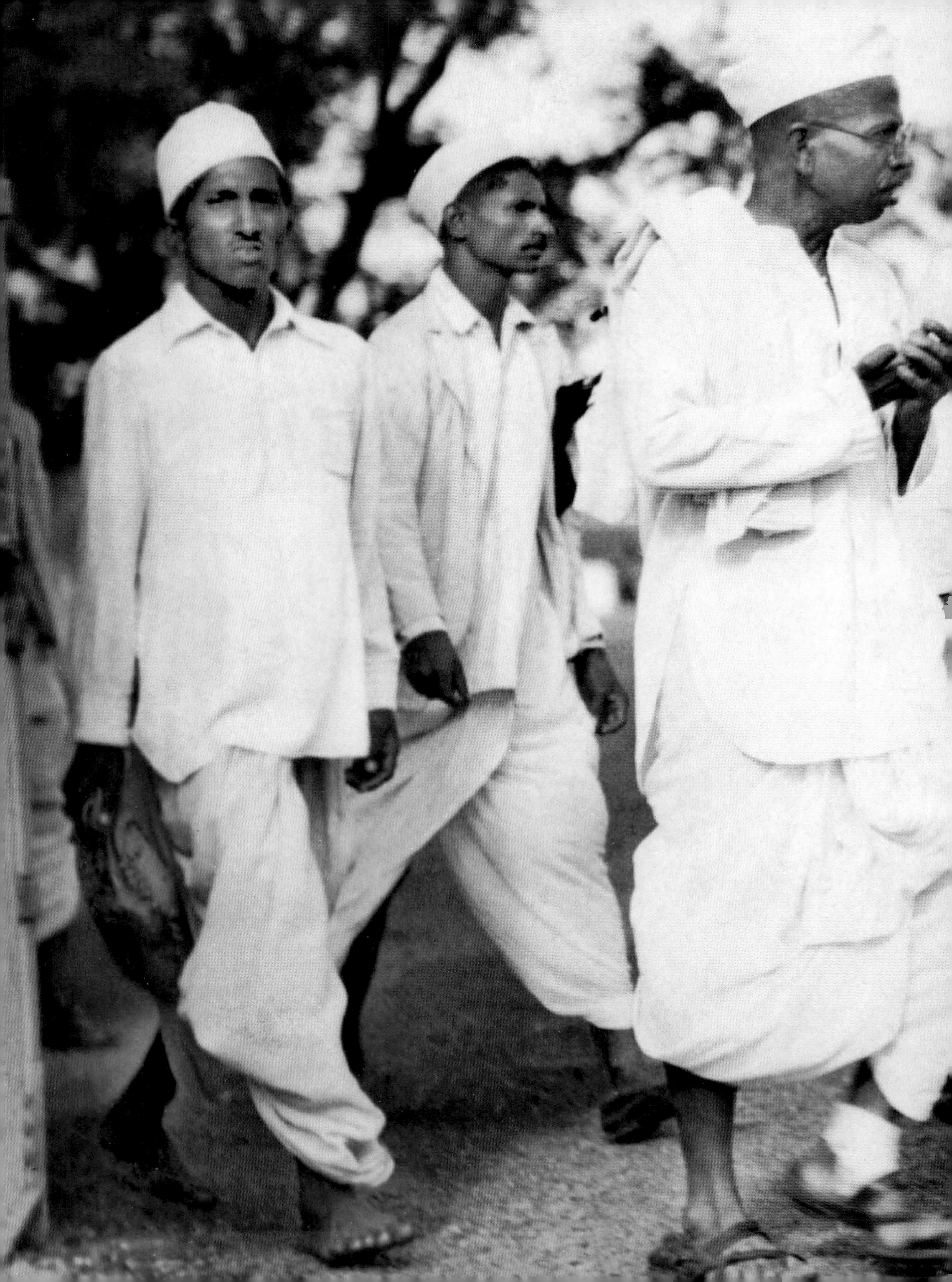

Gandhi attending a meeting of the Indian National Congress with his followers. *Wardha, India, 1937.*

[Please do] not look to my life, but take me even as a finger-post, a lamp-post on the road that indicates the way but cannot walk the way itself. I cannot present my life as an example.... Whomsoever you follow, howsoever great he might be, see to it that you follow the spirit of the master and not imitate him mechanically....

—Gandhi, *Young India, February 9, 1928*

...one thing took deep root in me—the conviction that morality is the basis of things, and that truth is the substance of all morality. Truth became my sole objective.It began to grow in magnitude every day....

—Gandhi, *Autobiography, The Story of My Experiments with Truth*

Introduction

This is the story of an extremely unusual revolutionary. Here you will read about a small, delicately-built man who nevertheless became a giant; about a person who possessed nothing and yet would leave an indelible imprint on human history. In a world wracked by violence, he proposed the way of *ahimsa*, or non-violence, while teaching the discovery of God and truth, respect for all human beings, and tolerance. Without ever raising his voice, he engaged his entire being in mobilizing the people of India in their fight for independence, and he succeeded. How was this possible? He succeeded because he possessed a great gift: the ability to speak to people's souls with the simplest words and gestures.

It was when he was in South Africa working as a young lawyer that he first decided to fight against racism and all other forms of exclusion. Returning to his country in 1915, he launched his first campaigns against the British. When he was tragically assass-inated in 1948, India had already won her independence thanks to his vision and his work.

But India's independence, though an enormous task, was only a part of his work. Above all, he whom the Indians called Mahatma (meaning Great Soul) aspired to "change hearts," for it was his belief that it is only through love that infinite possibilities are born. It is this task of changing hearts, which must be constantly accom-plished, that remains for us today. It is for this reason that Gandhi's message is addressed also to us and to those who will come after us. Let us listen to his words and consider whether some of his goals are also our own.

—E. de Lambilly

Gandhi playing with one of his children on the beach in Juho, near Bombay, c.1938.

Contents

12-22: Gandhi: Champion of Non-Violence
(A Biographical Comic)

23: Chronology

26: Gandhi's Life, His Struggles, His Faith

52: Gandhi: In His Own Words & Those of Others

66: Index

69: Bibliography & Recommended Reading

"To believe
not to live

Gandhi giving a speech to a
largely female crowd, 1938.

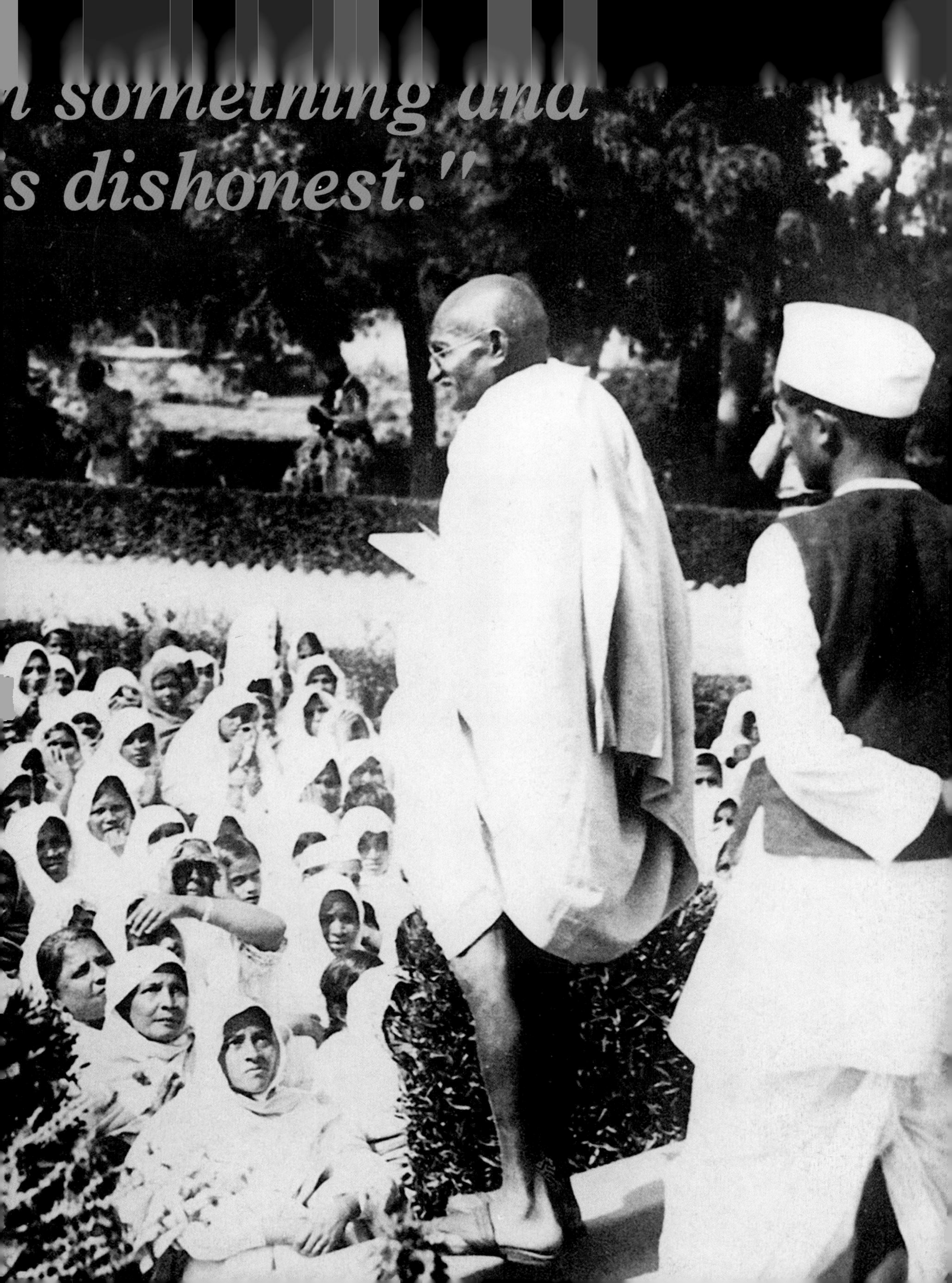
n something and
's dishonest."

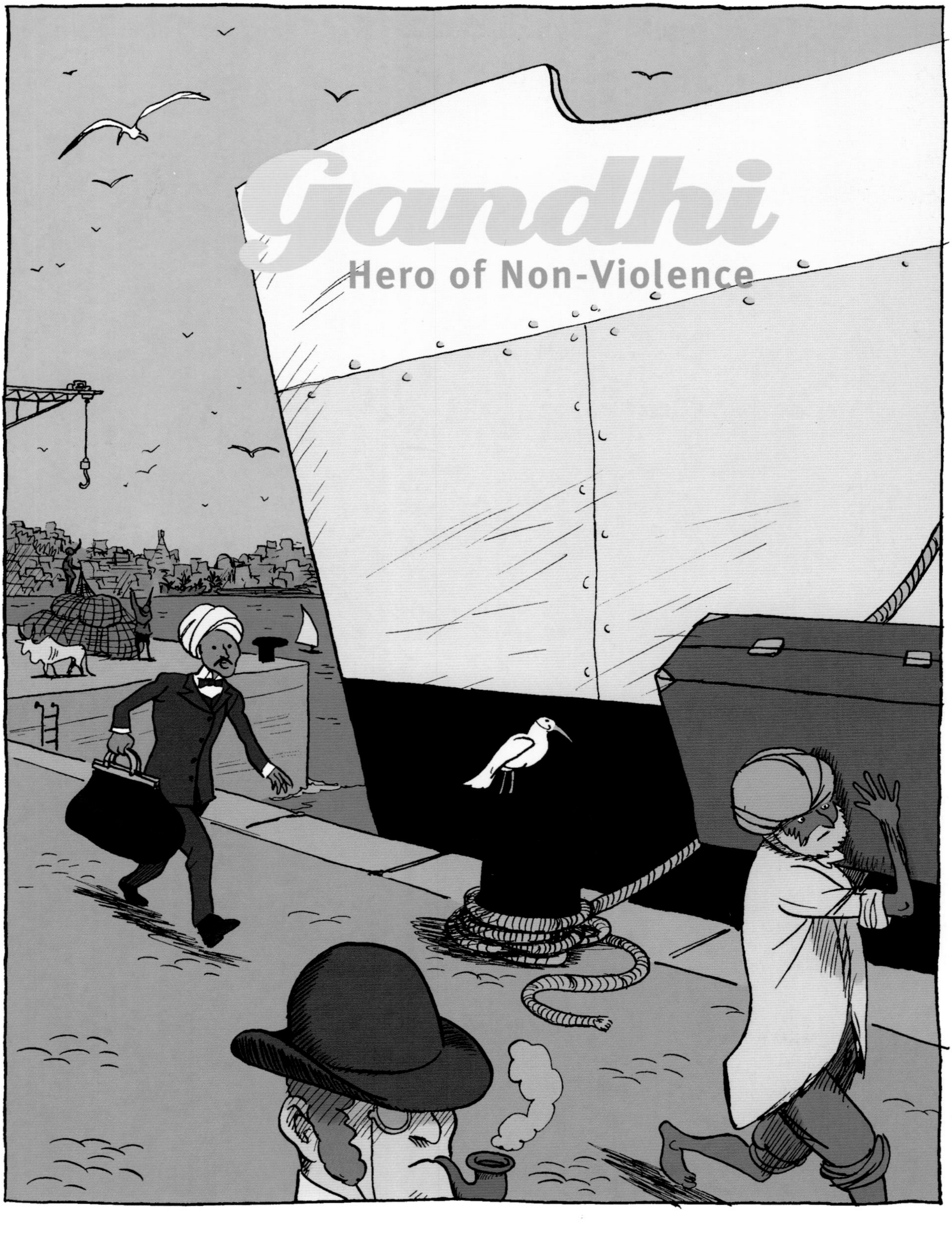
Gandhi
Hero of Non-Violence

* "Coolie" was originally used to refer to manual laborers from Asia, but quickly became a racial slur and an insult.

SEVERAL DAYS LATER AT THE HOME OF HIS NEW BOSS...

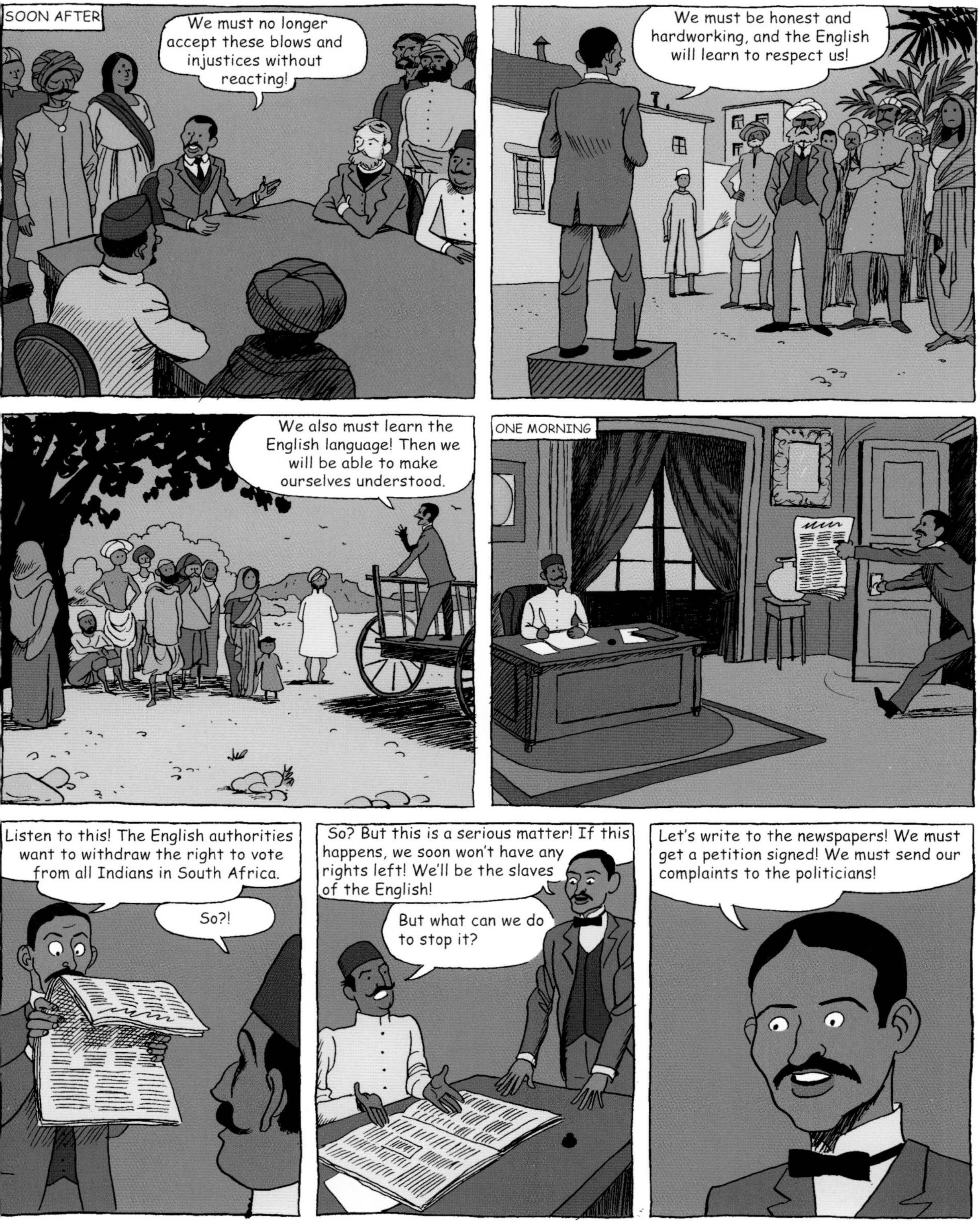
SOON AFTER
We must no longer accept these blows and injustices without reacting!
We must be honest and hardworking, and the English will learn to respect us!
We also must learn the English language! Then we will be able to make ourselves understood.
ONE MORNING
Listen to this! The English authorities want to withdraw the right to vote from all Indians in South Africa.
So?!
So? But this is a serious matter! If this happens, we soon won't have any rights left! We'll be the slaves of the English!
But what can we do to stop it?
Let's write to the newspapers! We must get a petition signed! We must send our complaints to the politicians!

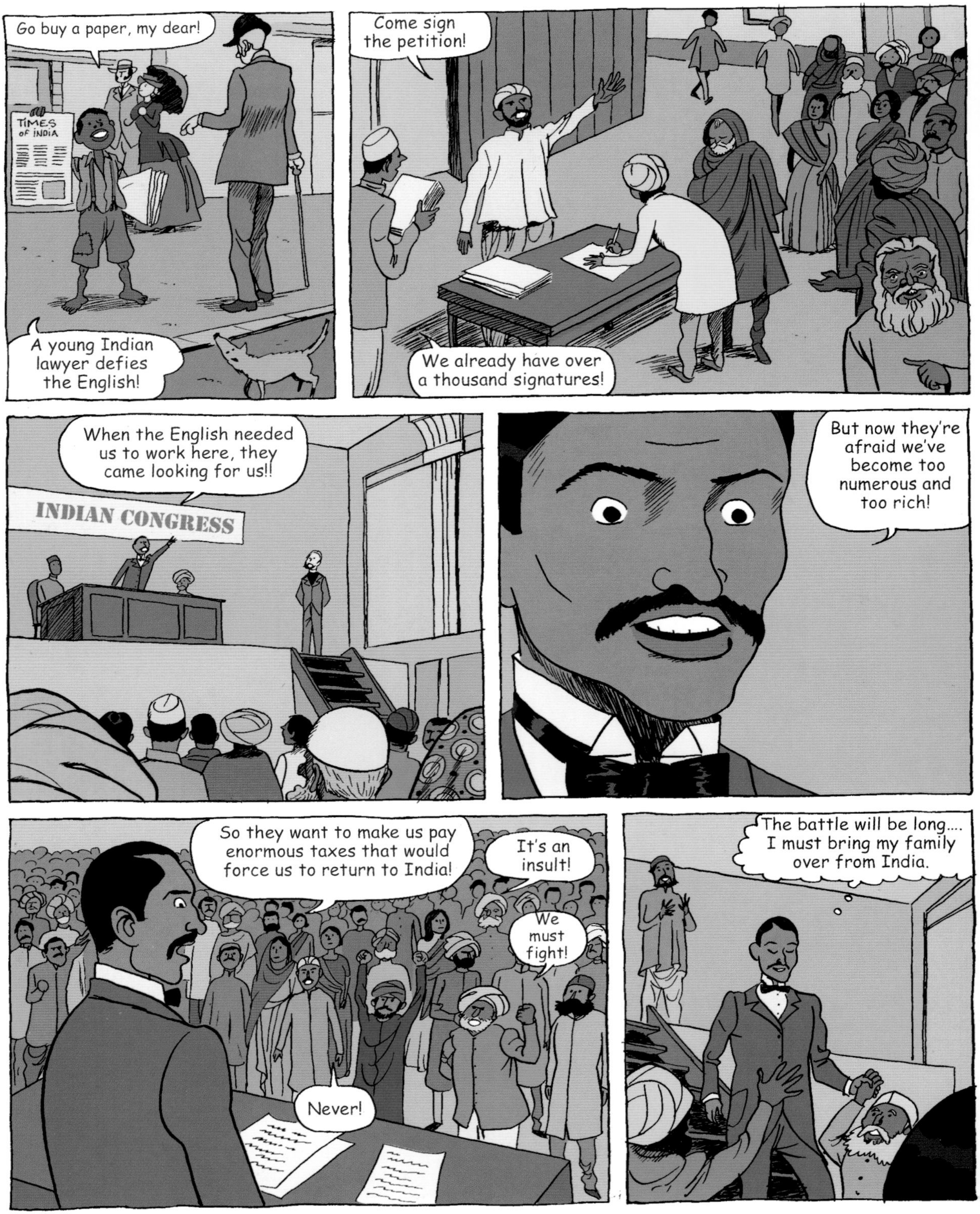
Go buy a paper, my dear!
TIMES OF INDIA
A young Indian lawyer defies the English!
Come sign the petition!
We already have over a thousand signatures!
When the English needed us to work here, they came looking for us!!
INDIAN CONGRESS
But now they're afraid we've become too numerous and too rich!
So they want to make us pay enormous taxes that would force us to return to India!
It's an insult!
We must fight!
Never!
The battle will be long.... I must bring my family over from India.

SEVERAL MONTHS LATER, IN 1896...

There's the port of Durban! We've arrived in South Africa, my children!

Yay!

What's happening, Mohandas?

I don't know...

Can we disembark, Captain?

No, we can't... and it's all because of you!

What do you mean?

The English are protesting your return, demanding that we go back to India along with all of the Indians aboard this boat!

Out of the question! We have the right to live in South Africa! We'll wait as long as it takes!

TWENTY-THREE DAYS LATER...

All right! You've won! You can all disembark!

17

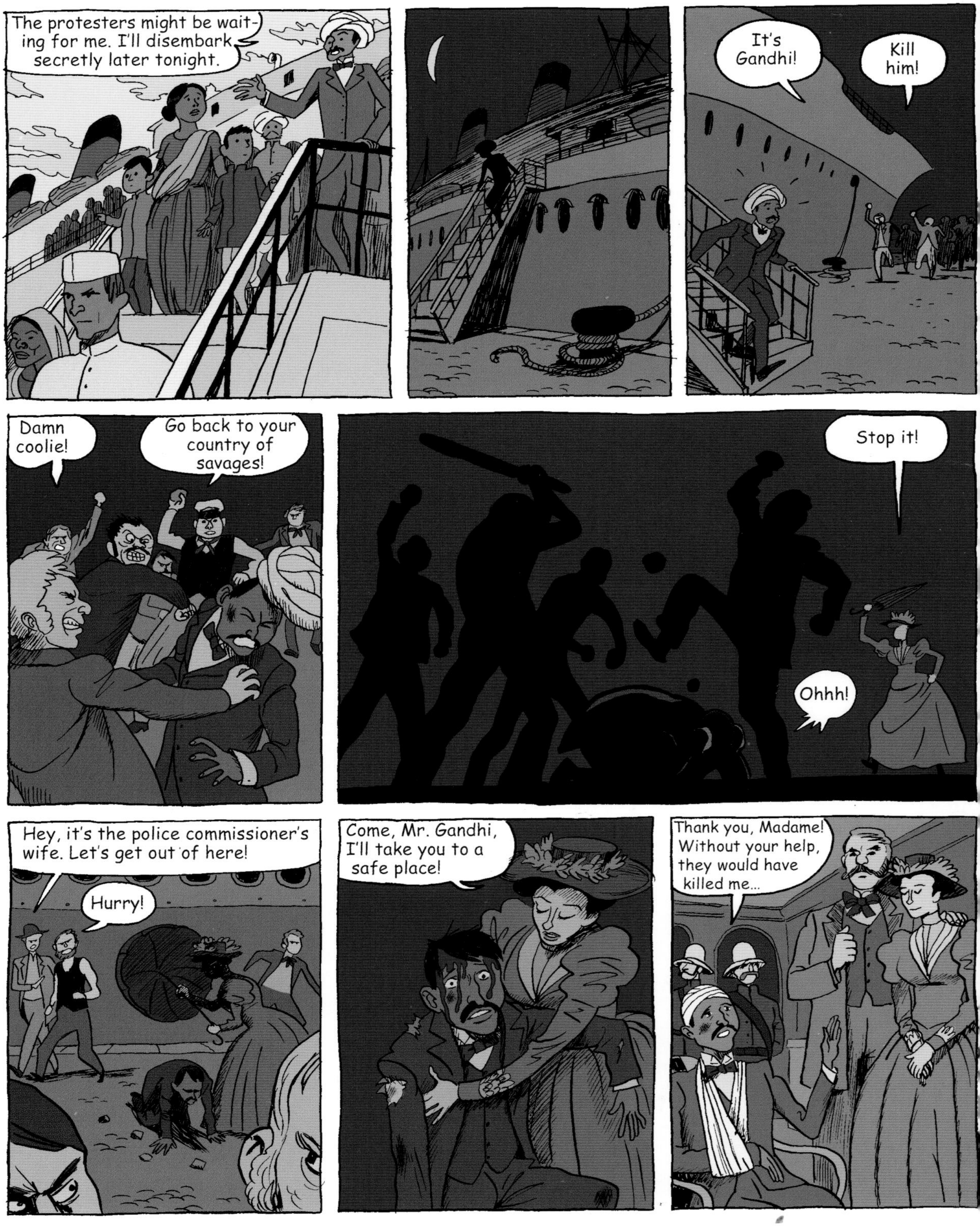
The protesters might be waiting for me. I'll disembark secretly later tonight.
It's Gandhi!
Kill him!
Damn coolie!
Go back to your country of savages!
Stop it!
Ohhh!
Hey, it's the police commissioner's wife. Let's get out of here!
Hurry!
Come, Mr. Gandhi, I'll take you to a safe place!
Thank you, Madame! Without your help, they would have killed me...

Gandhi resumed his career as a lawyer, continued his fight, formed an ashram,* and had two more sons. One day, in 1904...

What's wrong, Kasturba?

I don't understand you. First you make us leave our beautiful house for this god-forsaken hole, and now you won't even keep servants!

I have long dreamed of creating this ashram where we would be able to lead a simpler life.

This will bring us closer to God** and will help us to better serve the world.

I want to prove that people of different religions and cultures can live side by side!

Look Kasturba! Here at the newspaper office we have an English pastor, a German Jew, a Polish Catholic, a Muslim Indian, and me, a Hindu!

Here everyone must know how to cook, sew, garden, build, wash...

*In the Hindu religion an ashram is a place where people live communally, sharing everything.
**Hindus believe in the existence of many gods and that each god is a different representation of a single Supreme Being.

Yes, but cleaning the toilets is work fit only for the untouchables*!

No work is shameful. As for the untouchables, no one should be considered in this way anymore!

If we do not wish to be looked down upon, then we cannot look down on others.

If you disagree with this, leave!

You would cast me out? Me, who has always obeyed you without question!

I shouldn't have gotten angry... forgive me. I'll clean the toilets for you.

Wait! I'll go with you...

*In Hindu society the untouchables traditionally occupied the lowest place in the caste system. They were held to be impure and without caste and were forced to do the most undesireable jobs, like handling the dead and emptying toilets. From early on, Gandhi worked to abolish untouchability.

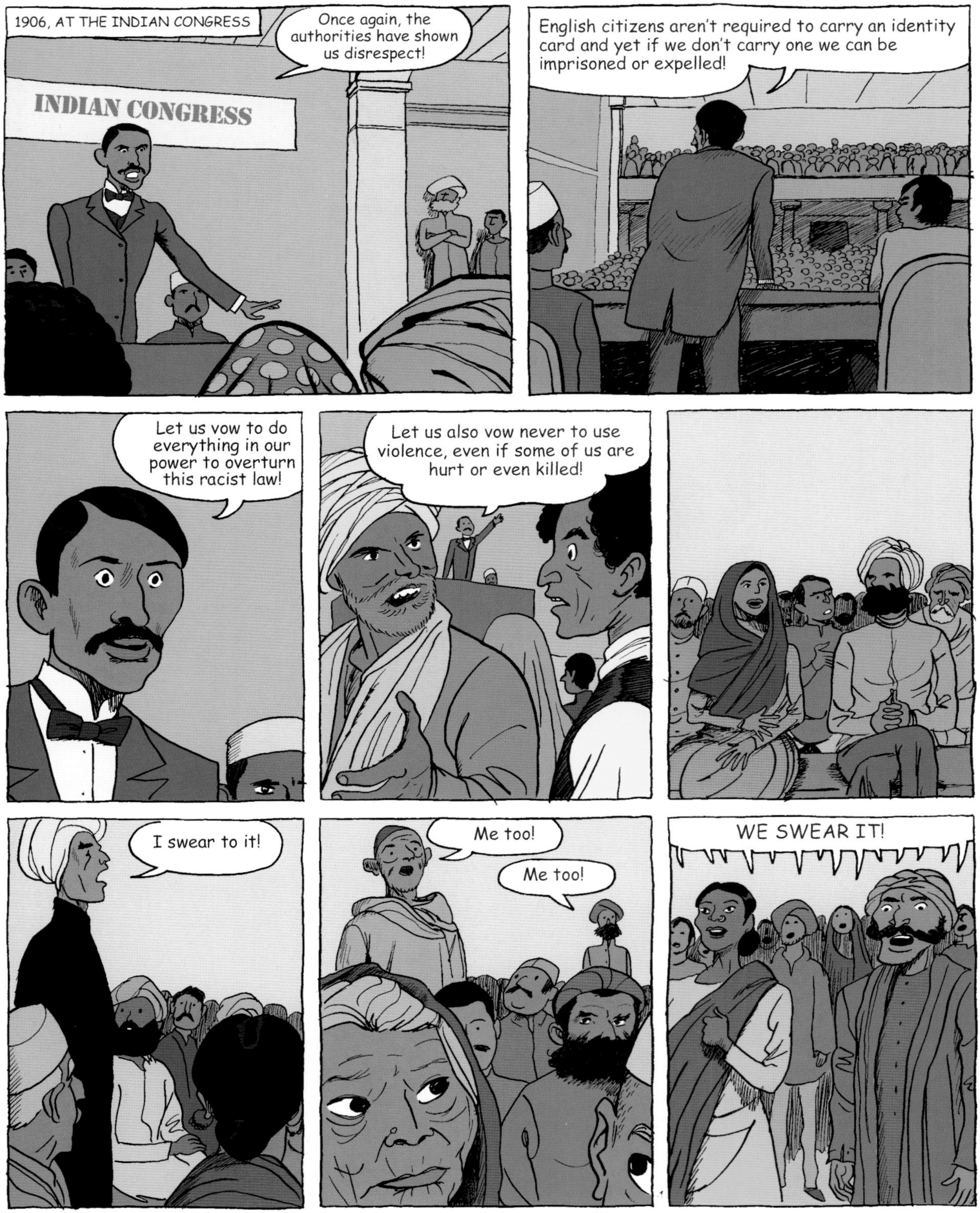
1906, AT THE INDIAN CONGRESS
Once again, the authorities have shown us disrespect!
INDIAN CONGRESS
English citizens aren't required to carry an identity card and yet if we don't carry one we can be imprisoned or expelled!
Let us vow to do everything in our power to overturn this racist law!
Let us also vow never to use violence, even if some of us are hurt or even killed!
I swear to it!
Me too!
Me too!
WE SWEAR IT!

1908... You have no identity card and you're inciting protests. I'm sending you to prison!

Non-violence is the only weapon we need in order to win. With it, we will fill their prisons...

We don't have identity cards either!

The prison is already full!

Put us in prison!

THE NON VIOLENT REBELLION GROWS...

CHARGE!

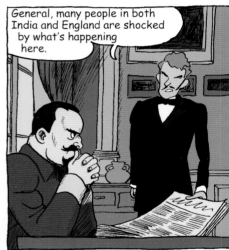

General, many people in both India and England are shocked by what's happening here.

Women and children killed during protests! Indians deported from South Africa ending up in poverty!

It would serve us better to free Gandhi and grant him his demands. This fragile, little man has beaten us!

Mr. Gandhi, you are free to go.

Layout : Benoît Marchon. Illustrations : Grégory Mardon. Color: Clémence Sapin.

Chronology

October 1869	Mohandas Karamchand Gandhi is born in Porbandar in the state of Gujarat.
1882	Gandhi marries Kasturba. Both are thirteen years old.
1885	Creation of the Indian National Congress
1888-1891	Gandhi is a law student in London
1893	Gandhi leaves for South Africa, where he will stay for 22 years.
1904	Creation of the first *ashram*, where work and life are communal.
September 11, 1906	Speech in Johannesburg in defense of the Indians of South Africa. Birth of the principle of *satyagraha*, or non-violence.
November 6, 1913	Gandhi's first non-violent action: the Transvaal March
January 1915	Return to India
April 1919	Gandhi proposes the first *hartal*, a day of prayer and fasting for the liberation of India.
April 13, 1919	The Amritsar Massacre
February 1922	Gandhi calls for civil disobedience
March 12 - April 6, 1930	The Salt March
1931	Gandhi is welcomed in London
1932	Gandhi fasts almost until death to defend the rights of the poor and the untouchables
August 1942	Gandhi launches the resolution "Quit India," hoping to hasten the departure of the English.
1944	Kasturba dies
1947	The move towards Indian independence incites numerous violent confrontations between Hindus and Muslims. Lord Mountbatten is named Viceroy to British India. He will be the last British Viceroy and Gandhi's faithful ally.
August 14, 1947	At midnight, Indian independence is proclaimed along with the birth of Pakistan, the first Muslim country in the world.
January 30, 1948	Gandhi is assassinated in Delhi by Nathuram Godse

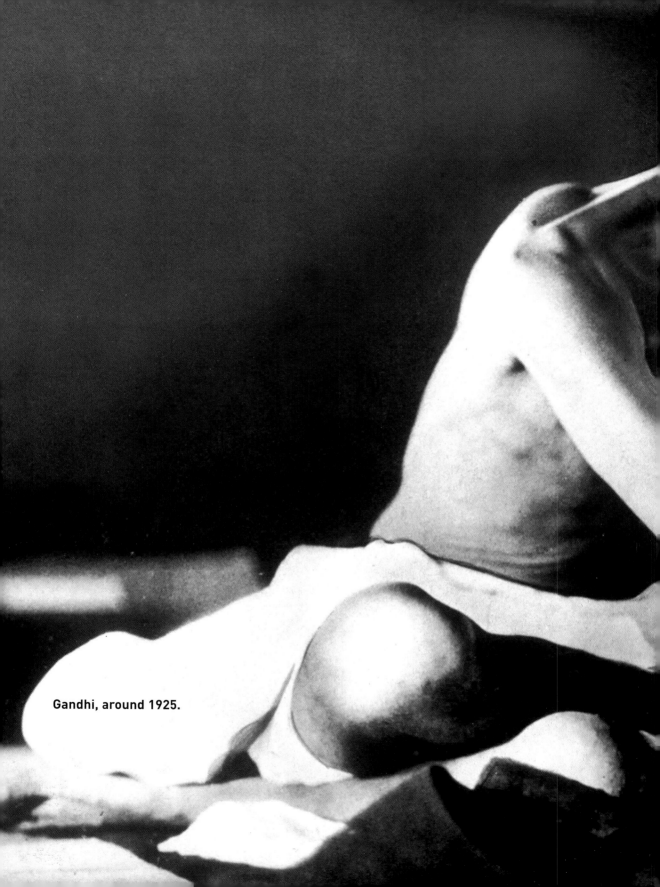

Gandhi, around 1925.

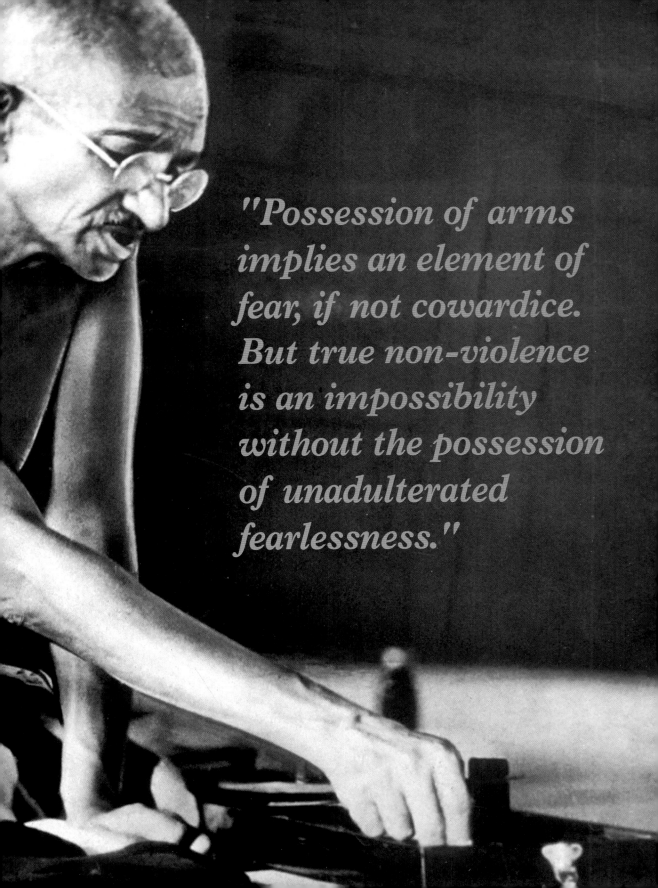

"Possession of arms implies an element of fear, if not cowardice. But true non-violence is an impossibility without the possession of unadulterated fearlessness."

The White City

It was in Porbandar, a port city of white houses on the Gulf of Oman to the north of Bombay (Mumbai today), that Gandhi was born on October 2, 1869. At the time India wasn't a free and independent country, but belonged to Britain's vast colonial empire. The immense Indian territory under British rule included a population of 350 million people, 179 languages, and 544 dialects.

Mohandas Gandhi was the last of four sons in a Hindu family. His father, whom he loved deeply, was "a lover of his clan, truthful, brave and generous, but short-tempered," as Gandhi later would write. He had received only a modest education, but still had the qualities to be Diwan (Prime Minister) of the tiny Princely State of Porbandar, a position held by his ancestors for six generations. The Gandhi family was well off despite belonging to the vaishya caste, which was fairly low in the Hindu social hierarchy. His mother was a dutiful wife and extremely devout. Like many Hindus, she was a vegetarian out of respect for all living creatures. She fasted regularly and prayed often, espousing tolerance and non-violence. In his *Autobiography* Gandhi writes "The outstanding impression my mother has left on my memory is that of saintliness."

As a little boy Gandhi was affectionately called Mohania. He was inquisitive and liked to explore the large family house, but he also was afraid of the dark and terrified of ghosts and snakes. At school he was shy and made few few friends, but he was curious about the natural world and liked to explore. His love for nature was in fact so strong that he once climbed up a mango tree that had lost a branch to bandage it. Similar qualities of strength and tenderness are revealed by the fact that his favorite childhood story was about Harishchandra, who endured tremendous hardship and sacrificed everything for his love of truth. This story from the Indian Epics captured Gandhi's heart, to the point that he cast himself into the role of Harishchandra again and again.

THE HINDU CASTE SYSTEM

Hindu society was divided into four main castes for thousands of years. At the top of the hierarchy were the Brahmins, scholars and priests who were held to have divine knowledge. Next came the kshatriyas, or warriors, who possessed military might, followed by the vaishyas, or merchants; this is the caste to which Gandhi's family belonged. Finally, there were the shudras, or the artisans and peasants. At the very bottom were those with no caste, called "untouchables." Considered impure, they were given only the most menial jobs. Although the Indian Constitution officially abolished the caste system in 1950, it continues to permeate Indian society even today.

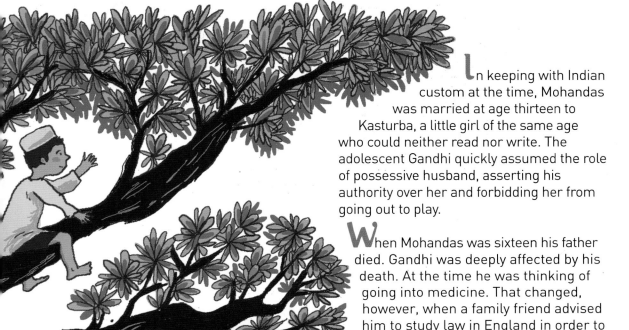

In keeping with Indian custom at the time, Mohandas was married at age thirteen to Kasturba, a little girl of the same age who could neither read nor write. The adolescent Gandhi quickly assumed the role of possessive husband, asserting his authority over her and forbidding her from going out to play.

When Mohandas was sixteen his father died. Gandhi was deeply affected by his death. At the time he was thinking of going into medicine. That changed, however, when a family friend advised him to study law in England in order to succeed his father as Diwan and support his family. His mother had her doubts, but Gandhi jumped at the chance.

Mohandas Gandhi and his brother Laxmidas in **1886.**

MANY LEAVES ON A SINGLE TREE

Six of the world's great religious communities intersected within British India. Among Indians, the majority of its inhabitants, the most widely practiced religion was Hinduism. For Hindus, God is present everywhere and has many representations. As for human beings, each is born into a caste that he or she can never leave. A Hindu's sole duty is ethical and honest conduct in the hope of a better life with the next reincarnation. The ultimate ideal and goal is to cease to be reborn. Other religions, such as Buddhism and Jainism, developed from Hinduism. Muslims lived alongside these communities (Islam was the second biggest religion in the region), as did Sikhs, Jews, Christians, and Parsis (sun worshippers from Persia). For Gandhi these many religions were like leaves on a single tree. Although each was different, they all had God as their trunk. As Gandhi described it, "Even as a tree has a single trunk, but many branches and leaves, there is one religion but any number of faiths."

London, 1888

THE SACRED BOOKS OF HINDUISM

The foundations of Hinduism are contained within the The Four Vedas and The Great Epics. The Vedas are a collection of stories about the Hindu gods, and instructions for hymns, rituals, prayers and sacrifice that were passed down orally over thousands of years. The Great Epics are marvelous tales recounting the great deeds of a hero or a group. The first of these is the *Mahabharata*, a poem of nearly 100,000 verses, which includes the *Bhagavad Gita*, or the "Song of God," one of the three holiest scriptures of Hinduism. The *Bhagavad Gita* is a series of ethical discourses between Lord Krishna and the warrior Prince Arjuna from which the essential teachings of Indian philosophy derive. Arjuna is poised to announce the start of combat on the battlefield, but noticing people whom he cares for on both sides, he realizes that some of his loved ones will perish. Krishna, an incarnation of the god Vishnu, teaches Arjuna that war is an allegory for the inner confusion and conflict that affects everyone at some point in his or her life. True peace, he further instructs, can only be found through meditation, selflessness and a search for truth.

Gandhi as a young lawyer in Western clothes on his arrival in South Africa in 1893.

Godless London

Leaving India was not easy. Gandhi's mother was worried, convinced that London was an immoral den of vice where her son would forget the principles of his religion. Mohandas thus vowed to her that he would not consort with women, eat meat, or drink alcohol. Moreover, since traveling overseas was contrary to the traditions of his caste, he was summoned before his caste's leaders, who tried to get him to hear reason. But Gandhi stood his ground, and thus on September 4, 1888, shortly before his departure, he was solemnly expelled from his caste. With that, he left for the teeming city of Bombay, from where he would sail for Britain.

Gandhi felt lost in London. He found the city enormous, cold, and gray. He could barely speak English and didn't even know how to use a fork. His goal thus became flawless adaptation: he would become a perfect English gentleman. However, after a few months of dutifully learning to tie a tie, wax his hair, and dance, he realized the futility of his efforts. It wasn't just the thought that he was there for only a short time and had more to do than waltzing and grooming that changed things. What became clear to him was that he was different from the British, and he would never be one of them, no matter how hard he tried. Moreover, his money was running out and he needed to lower his expenses. As he explored different avenues and pondered his identity as an Indian from the British colonies in London, he became serious about his studies and immersed himself in reading. He also became a serious vegetarian.

It was in this way that thousands of miles from home, Gandhi began to make the emotional discovery of his own identity, culture and religion. He also discovered one of his own religion's major scriptures, the *Bhagavad Gita.* As Gandhi later would write, "...to me the *Gita* became an infallible guide of conduct. It became my dictionary of daily reference." In other words, it took going to England for Gandhi to understand himself as an Indian. He also began to read the *Bible* and the *Koran* and was deeply moved by Jesus' teachings from the *New Testament.* He found the idea of selflessness as the highest form of all religious practice enormously compelling.

In 1891, with his law degree in hand, Gandhi boarded a boat and returned home. Once there, after much thought, he decided to open a law office in Bombay. His first case was a bitter failure, with nerves getting the better of him, and business was bad. Although his quiet voice would one day inspire an entire people, he was still too awkward and shy to speak in public. Desperate to make a living and to provide for his family, he thus accepted a position in South Africa to represent a distant cousin in a civil suit. With sorrow, he left Kasturba and his two sons behind.

Gandhi planned to spend only a few months in South Africa, but he ended up staying for twenty-two crucial years that formed the core of his personality. As he himself described it, "I went there seeking my fortune, and instead I found a search for God and self-realization." Like India, South Africa belonged to the British Empire, and it was there, in that colonial atmosphere, that he would experience the most decisive moment of his life.

That moment arrived when Gandhi went by train from Durban to Pretoria to work on a case. He was dressed in fine European clothes and took his seat in the first-class car. When a white man who boarded the train at the Maritzburg station saw that an Indian was sitting in the section where he was to sit, he called over the conductor and demanded that the "dirty coolie" be removed. Gandhi refused to leave and showed his first-class ticket, but it was no use, and he was thrown off the train. It was a cold night, and as Gandhi sat shivering on a bench in deep despair he pondered the situation of his people in South Africa. As dawn broke he made the most important decision of his entire life. He decided that he would never again accept injustice. It was June 7, 1893, and Gandhi was 25. "This is how God built the foundations of the life I would lead in South Africa, and sowed the seeds of the struggle for national dignity," he later would write.

A few days later the young timid lawyer made his first speech before the Indians of Pretoria. He asked them to unite and stand up for themselves. Their agreement was immediate and unified. Gandhi's first victory came when he won the right for appropriately dressed Indians to travel first class. Success followed success and within a year Gandhi had become a prosperous lawyer for the Indian community. With his goal accomplished, he prepared to return home. But when he learned of a measure that would deny the Indians in South Africa the right to vote, he changed his mind. He could not abandon the fight. Sensing that the struggle would be long, he traveled home for Kasturba and his children.

Indian workers in the sugar cane fields.

Rejecting Injustice

When Gandhi returned to Durban his ship was quarantined. The European community there was unhappy about his return because of the newspaper articles he had written about them back home in India. Their demand was for Gandhi and his family to be repatriated, along with all of the other unwanted Indians on the boat. As far as they were concerned Gandhi had caused enough trouble already. The Indian community prevailed and the boat was not sent back, but weeks later, when Gandhi finally disembarked under cover of night, a riot broke out. Without the courageous intervention of the police chief's wife, Gandhi would have been beaten to death. The government in London ordered his assailants to be brought to justice, but Gandhi publicly refused to prosecute. He preferred to act on his belief that vengeance is not the way to disarm one's enemies. His decision not to prosecute won him increased respect among Indians and Europeans alike and was taken note of in London as well.

INDIANS IN SOUTH AFRICA

The English living in South Africa and the Boers (colonists of Dutch origin) were dissatisfied with their African workers. They thus turned to Britain's colonial empire for labor. Indians, mostly untouchables, came by the thousands to work on their farms and sugar plantations. These Indians were called "coolies" (originally a Hindi word meaning "porter"), and once their contract was up many of them settled permanently in South Africa. Some of the Indians who came were businessmen or merchants, but to racist white South Africans they could never be more than coolies. The Indians were thus subject to many racist and unjust laws.

Renunciation

andhi's struggle for his people in South Africa profoundly changed him. As a young law student he had read in the *Bhagavad Gita* that renunciation was essential for spiritual awakening. This idea stayed with him and moved him in deep ways. Over time he began to see renunciation as the only way to move closer to God and little by little he began to change. First he abandoned his suits and ties in favor of a white cotton Indian tunic with a matching cap. He further embraced asceticism by learning to do his own laundry and even clean his own toilet, a task traditionally reserved for untouchables. He also pared down his life by eating only once a day and fasting regularly.

But it was a book by John Ruskin, which he devoured in one sitting on an overnight train in 1904, that led him to complete his transformation. The book was *Unto This Last,* in which Ruskin, an English art critic and philosopher, denounces wealth as a cause of slavery. He then shows how a life of manual labor is the only kind of life worth living. Interestingly, both Gandhi and Dr. Martin Luther King, Jr. cited this book as a powerful influence. As Gandhi wrote, "The book was impossible to lay aside, once I had begun it. It gripped me…. I could not get any sleep that night. I determined to change my life in accordance with the ideals of the book." Gandhi's words about Tolstoy (see box) can be applied to Ruskin as well: "What has appealed to me most in Tolstoy's life is that he praticed what he preached."

Gandhi and his wife Kasturba

The First Ashram.

and Selflessness

Gandhi decided to give up all luxury from then on. This might have been a simple decision had Gandhi not had a family and a good income. He realized that it would be hard on his wife and children. Certain, however, that he was making the right decision, he threw himself into changing his life. After searching for just the right place, he brought his wife and four sons, as well as a small group of friends, into the middle of the countryside. Their destination was a broken-down shack surrounded by a harsh landscape with a few mango trees among the snake-infested brambles. This was the first ashram, a place of quiet reflection, prayer, and communal living, where everyone shared everything. Kasturba, despite some mis-givings, accepted this new life, and soon afterward, Gandhi took the vow of *brahmacharya*, a Hindu religious practice that allows men who are of sufficient age, and who have already procreated, to be celibate.

LEO TOLSTOY

Gandhi admired the ideas of Leo Tolstoy, the great Russian writer, who sought to apply the strictures of Christianity to his daily life. As Gandhi put it, "What has appealed to me most in Tolstoy's life is that he practiced what he preached and reckoned no cost too great in his pursuit of truth." In his book, *The Kingdom of God Is Within You*, Tolstoy writes that love and compassion have the power to transform humanity. Gandhi and Tolstoy shared the same view on non-violence and wrote to each other up until Tolstoy's death in 1910. Gandhi founded a second ashram in South Africa that same year, naming it Tolstoy Farm in honor of his friend.

Satyagraha: the

Gandhi had long meditated on non-violence. Although it was a widespread concept in India and one with which he had grown up, his belief in it was deepened through his reading of the Gospels. He was profoundly affected by the teachings of Christ, who said that instead of responding to a blow with a blow, one should always turn the other cheek, returning hatred with love. Gandhi knew that violence would always lead to more violence. Thus, while he firmly believed in civil disobedience and in resisting unjust laws, he was certain that such refusal had to be expressed without violence. He was convinced that un-wavering non-violent resistance had the power to uphold human dignity and disarm even the most formidable adversary.

Gandhi first put his theory into practice in Johannesburg in 1906. One night he spoke before an angry crowd of thousands to denounce a law that would deny the right of residency to any Indian, age eight or older, who had not been fingerprinted and documented by the police. This was a new blow to his community, and Gandhi saw only one solution: *"resistance unto death rather than submission."* They would resist, but they would resist and be beaten. They would not react. One by one the many Indians in the crowd agreed to follow his example and solemnly swore to disobey without violence. With that action, Gandhi laid the groundwork for a new form of political action through non-violent resist-ance. He called it *satyagraha—satya* meaning "truth," and *graha* meaning "force" or "firmness." Gandhi thus became the first person to use non-violence in

politics. Later, a number of great men, such as Martin Luther King, Jr., would follow his example.

Year after year, the satyagraha move-ment grew. Strikes and protests multiplied, and thousands of Indians were crammed into South African jails. In 1913, Gandhi spoke out when the State of Transvaal (a South African province at the time) decided to close its borders to Indians. Leading a crowd of over two thousand people, Gandhi marched toward the forbidden territory where soldiers waited, armed to the teeth.

As he stood before the calm resolution of his supporters, Gandhi saw the power of non-violent action on a grand scale. He was once again thrown into prison, but he was quickly released due to his popu-larity. The Governor of the Transvaal agreed to negotiate, and so Gandhi once again succeeded in winning rights for his people. His South African mission ended in victory.

Power of Truth

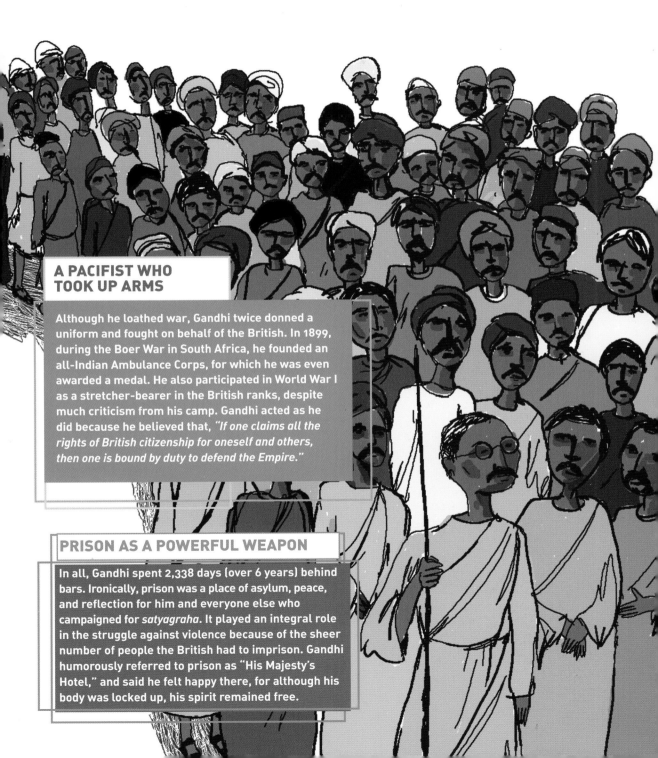

A PACIFIST WHO TOOK UP ARMS

Although he loathed war, Gandhi twice donned a uniform and fought on behalf of the British. In 1899, during the Boer War in South Africa, he founded an all-Indian Ambulance Corps, for which he was even awarded a medal. He also participated in World War I as a stretcher-bearer in the British ranks, despite much criticism from his camp. Gandhi acted as he did because he believed that, *"If one claims all the rights of British citizenship for oneself and others, then one is bound by duty to defend the Empire."*

PRISON AS A POWERFUL WEAPON

In all, Gandhi spent 2,338 days (over 6 years) behind bars. Ironically, prison was a place of asylum, peace, and reflection for him and everyone else who campaigned for *satyagraha*. It played an integral role in the struggle against violence because of the sheer number of people the British had to imprison. Gandhi humorously referred to prison as "His Majesty's Hotel," and said he felt happy there, for although his body was locked up, his spirit remained free.

The Message of Silence

When Gandhi arrived in Bombay on January 9, 1915, he was welcomed by an enormous, cheering crowd. After being away for so many years, Gandhi's deepest wish was that he would get to know the people of his homeland. For almost a year after his return, he traveled through the vast expanse of his country. He went from village to village, traveling long distances either on foot or by train as a third-class passenger. He was outraged by the filth and ignorance that he encountered and quickly realized that the Indian people would have to reclaim their history and culture in order to become independent. Each individual would also have to learn to respect all people, including the untouchables and the despised British, to be worthy of freedom.

With his beliefs stronger and clearer than ever, Gandhi founded a community on the banks of the Sabarmati River in Porbandar, the place of his birth. There, despite general outrage, he did something unheard of: he allowed a family of untouchables to live in his ashram. As always, his focus was on the enormous task of helping the vulnerable and the oppressed, and once again he aimed to do this through right action. At the ashram Gandhi got down to work, and he gave everything to his cause. He headed up thousands of peasants to denounce their exploitation; he held a public fast in favor of textile workers who demanded a salary increase; and he assisted peasants decimated by drought who refused to pay the British tax. It was during this period of intense activism that the great Indian poet and philosopher Rabindranath Tagore gave Gandhi the name Mahatma, meaning "Great Soul."

THE ENGLISH IN INDIA

The lands that comprised British India officially became a colony of the British Empire in 1858. Along with their customs the British brought their institutions and their language, which eventually would become a unifying force for the many different groups, with their many different dialects, within British India. Convinced of their superiority, the British had very little contact with the population under their rule. They socialized in clubs that were closed to Indians; held large banquets with only British food; and played tennis, polo and cricket among themselves. Most whites at that time did not believe that the Indian population had the right to live with the dignity and respect that comes with equality and freedom.

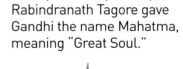

The Indian police disperse a demonstration of Gandhi's followers **around 1919**.

Gandhi directly confronted the British Empire for the first time in April 1919 at the age of 43. England had resolved through the Rowlatt Act to ruthlessly repress any demonstration in favor of Indian independence and to imprison those accused of sedition without trial. Gandhi carefully considered how to protest the Act. Finally, the solution came to him in a dream. He would call for an all-India *hartal*, a day of fasting and prayer: *"May all India stop what it's doing so that its oppressors can hear the message of its silence."* Gandhi and his followers spread the news, and Indians everywhere enthusiastically answered the call. On the chosen day, stores were closed, schools were deserted, and factories stopped. Silent gatherings formed across the land.

At times, however, non-violence can lead to violence, and on April 13, 1919, in Punjab, English machine guns fired into the defenseless crowd, killing over three hundred people in what came to be known as the Amritsar Massacre. Enraged, many Indians engaged in retaliatory acts against the British. When Gandhi heard the news he was heartbroken, and he blamed both the British and the Indians. He held himself responsible for the failure of his followers and suspended the *satyagraha* movement.

The Amritsar Massacre led Gandhi to lose his faith in the British Empire for good. From then on he devoted all of his energy to winning India's independence. In 1920, he became one of the main leaders of the Indian National Congress and launched a plan of action. Once again his idea was astonishingly simple and everyone — young and old; Hindus, Sikhs, and Muslims; intellectuals and illiterate peasants — understood it.

What Gandhi proposed was non-cooperation, by which he meant a refusal to participate in anything British. He asked for parents to no longer send their children to English schools, for students to no longer attend class at university, for lawyers to leave their tribunals, for bureaucrats to abandon their jobs, and for everybody to refuse to pay taxes. In a symbolic gesture, Gandhi even returned his military decorations to the Viceroy. Above all he went after

The Spinning wheel not the Sword

Gandhi spinning cotton, **1931**

the textile industry since it brought considerable profit to the British. In the colonial system, Indian peasants were compelled to plant cotton, which then was purchased at a very low price by the British and sent to England. There it was manufactured into clothing that was then sold back to India at exorbitant prices. To reject the injustice of this system, Gandhi armed himself with the spinning wheel, an ancestral tool that spins cotton into thread. Indians throughout British India followed Gandhi's example and took to spinning. Gandhi devoted a half hour each day to his spinning wheel, praying as he spun. When Congress members met for work, the clicking of spinning wheels made up the background noise.

Before long, Gandhi solemnly declared that he would wear nothing more than a hand-made loincloth and a wrap. Urging action, Gandhi and his followers organized the burning of clothes that had been made in England. Everywhere enormous piles of clothing were burned. Social unrest became widespread, and over thirty thousand Indians were thrown into prison. On February 1, 1922, Gandhi warned the Viceroy that he would intensify his actions, and that this time they would involve the outright rejection of British rule. Thousands of Indians answered his call to civil disobedience. Tragically, this initially non-violent refusal of British rule ended with an appalling episode in the village of Chauri Chaura, not far from New Delhi, when police officers were burned alive by a hate-filled crowd. Horrified, Gandhi suspended the movement. Clearly those who followed him had not understood his ideal of non-violence. Gandhi was arrested a few days later, and when he was brought before the judge, he delivered a passionate indictment against himself and requested the most severe punishment. He was condemned to six years in prison.

Gandhi in prison.

THE INDIAN NATIONAL CONGRESS

In 1885, a few educated Indians founded the Indian National Congress as a discussion group, with the goal of opening up the government of India to the Indian elite without undermining the British presence there. In fact, the movement's leader was himself an Englishman! It wasn't until after World War I, under Gandhi's influence, that the idea of independence really took hold and the Congress became a true nationalist political party. The Congress remains one of the major political parties in India to this day.

A Pinch of Independence

Gandhi was freed after two years in prison. Now 52, he remained irrepressible. Once again, he set out to see his country, this time supported by a bamboo cane. Crowds from all over rushed to see him, to hear him speak, and to touch him. From one gathering to the next, he once again became the voice of non-violence as the only road to Indian independence. He also advocated against child marriage, protested the exclusion of untouchables, and pleaded for reconciliation between Hindus and Muslims. Although the young Indian nationalists continued to support him, they were beginning to grow impatient at the continuing presence of the English. Attacks multiplied and by the end of 1929, Gandhi asked Congress members to swear an oath that they would win India's total independence non-violently, whatever the cost. The Congress agreed. The struggle for independence had officially begun, but Gandhi knew that it could not be won without the full support of the people behind him. He also knew that for non-violence to work he needed a practical plan.

Through silent meditation Gandhi arrived at a simple but powerful act of civil disobedience involving salt. Salt slows dehydration, making it an essential ingredient in an area as hot as India, but its sale had been monopolized and taxed by the English since the beginning of

Salt for

A moment of intimacy between Nehru and Gandhi.

colonial rule. India needed to regain her right to sell her own salt. Before sunrise on March 12, 1930, after an intense period of organization, Gandhi took to the road with his disciples, including Jawaharlal Nehru, one of his most trusted companions. This small group marched "in the name of God" towards the sea, gaining followers at every village. Twenty-six days later the procession reached the shores of the Gulf of Oman. As thousands of Indians and journalists from all over the world watched, Gandhi scooped up a handful of salt from the shore and held it briefly in his fist before presenting it to the crowd. His gesture was a symbol of freedom, asserting Indian ownership of the salt and the land. It was at this moment that Gandhi's struggle became known throughout the entire world. At age 61, he became a player on the world stage, and Indians thought of him not only as Mahatma, but also as Bapu, or "Grandfather."

For one week salt was illegally harvested and sold. Then the British acted. Gandhi was arrested along with nearly sixty thousand others, but the British Empire had been shaken. Behind bars once again, Gandhi relayed a message to his followers: *"The fist that held the salt can be broken, but the salt will never be returned."*

JAWAHARLAL NEHRU, THE MAN WITH THE ROSE LAPEL

Nehru, whom Gandhi claimed to love as a son, was born into a Brahmin family from Kashmir. At age 16, he was sent to study in England, where he became a lawyer. Upon returning to India he joined his father in the Congress Party. He was charming, elegant and always wore a rose in his lapel. He was quickly elected as Congress president, a post he held for three consecutive terms, thanks to his extensive education and his talents as a writer and a speaker. Like Gandhi, he was driven by a desire to see India become independent, and soon after their meeting in 1916, he became one of Gandhi's closest collaborators despite the fact that the two men had little else in common. Gandhi was as attached to religion and tradition as Nehru was to atheism and his belief in progress and science. Yet Nehru joined with Gandhi and, like him, made numerous visits to jail. In 1947 Nehru was elected Prime Minister of India, a position he held until his death in 1964.

While Gandhi was in jail, the salt battle continued. In May 1930 his son Manilal headed up a dramatic operation when he marched with 2,500 unarmed volunteers to the Dharasana salt factory. Police guarding the area had been ordered to stop the Indians from entering, and the demonstrators were beaten with clubs as they silently approached. Women helped those who fell and tended to their wounds, while a new row of men immediately stepped up to take a beating. A journalist who witnessed the scene was deeply sickened by it. The very next day newspapers all over the world reported what had happened and declared that India, having taken the high moral ground against the British, could now call herself free.

The Indian Viceroy, Lord Irwin, understood that he had to negotiate with Gandhi, so he had him released from prison and invited him to his palace in New Delhi. Winston Churchill, the future Prime Minister of Britain, also understood what was at stake in the meeting and was furious that the "half-naked fakir" received treatment worthy of a head of state. Three weeks later, the highest British authority on Indian soil and the barefooted Gandhi signed a pact as equals in a tremendous victory for Gandhi. The Viceroy freed all prisoners and authorized the sale of sea salt. In exchange, Gandhi agreed to suspend his movement and attend a conference in London on the future of India.

Freedom's

Forty-three years after his first visit, Gandhi returned to London. Dressed, as always, in a cotton loincloth and a wrap, he drank tea with the king and queen, answered reporters' questions, and joked with the crowds that had gathered to see him. He was honored and welcomed wherever he went, but he refused lodging at the palaces offered to him, choosing instead to stay among the poor in a lower-class neighborhood. Unfortunately, the conference was an utter failure, and the discussions went nowhere. England was not yet ready to let India go. All that remained was for Gandhi to return home to India where he was needed.

TRAVELING LIGHT

A small bundle of items, carried wherever he went, was all that Gandhi possessed. He had a clay bowl and a wooden spoon, his spinning wheel and some cotton, a dozen or so scraps of paper, and pencil stubs that he used till they were gone out of respect for the workers who made them. He also carried the *Bhagavad Gita*, the *Bible*, and the *Koran*, and a small ivory figurine of the three monkeys, one with its hands over its eyes, one with hands over its ears, and the third with its hands over its mouth, recalling the three secrets of wisdom: *"hear no evil, see no evil, speak no evil."*

Messenger

On his arrival in England, Gandhi made a tour of the cotton factories in Lancashire. Here he is being cheered by the female workers of the factory in Darweed in **1931**.

Gandhi left a profound impression on Europe. People were intrigued by his message of love and peace. Later he would write that this was undoubtedly because he chose a unique method for winning freedom, and that *"the world [was] sick unto death of blood-spilling."*

When Gandhi returned to India he learned that Nehru and the other Congress members had been arrested, and that the liberties he had won for his people had been scaled back. The new viceroy refused any negotiation and, less than a month after his triumphant return, Gandhi was once again thrown into jail.

It's not my Life that Matters

Gandhi on his mat.

From generation to generation, the untouchables had lived at the very bottom of the social hierarchy. They were thought of as impure and were responsible for the most degrading jobs. Upper-caste Hindus had to avoid all contact with them for fear of being polluted. They thus were forced to live in poverty on the outskirts of villages, where their children roamed the unsanitary streets. But for Gandhi the untouchables were *harijan*, or children of God, like everybody else. Removing untouchability and the stain it put on the Hindu faith was thus part of his lifelong dream. Gandhi was in prison when he learned that each of the different religious communities, as well as the untouchables, would vote separately under the new constitution that England was drawing up. This troubled him greatly since it was deeply unjust to have the untouchables, already outcasts, vote as a distinct group. Conseqeuently, on September 20, 1932, Gandhi, now 65, announced from his prison cell that he would fast until death to gain respect for the untouchables. *"What I want, what I live for, and what I would be very happy to die for, is the complete disappearance of untouchability. My life doesn't matter."*

It was not long before all of India heard the news, and soon the whole country began to pray. Upper-caste Hindus publicly broke the taboo of accepting

food from the hands of untouchables, and temples opened their doors to the former outcasts. In Bombay, Hindu leaders gathered together and frantically discussed how to save Bapu's life, while daily updates about his health were distributed throughout the country. On September 24, Hindus and untouchables signed an agreement that came to be known as the London Agreement. Although Gandhi received the news with satisfaction, he refused to eat before seeing the document himself. The package arrived on the morning of September 26, and Gandhi, now near death, finally broke his fast. Indians had answered his call, forcefully weakening practices that had dominated Indian society for thousands of years. It was an astonishing victory.

When World War II broke out, Gandhi, who was 70, was a committed radical pacifist. In August 1942, to prevent India's participation in the war, Gandhi launched the "Quit India" campaign, and he asked the British to leave "this very night, before dawn." But before dawn arrived, Gandhi and all the members of the Congress were thrown into prison, where Kasturba would die following a bout of bronchitis. Gandhi too fell sick in prison, but he was released in satisfactory health in May 1944. Weakened by the war, England was now resigned to India's independence. No one had yearned for this more than Gandhi, but when it came, it came in a way that pained him deeply.

Nehru

Gandhi

The Congress's opposing political party was the Muslim League, which represented Muslim Indians. Its leader, Muhammad Ali Jinnah, wanted the creation of an autonomous Muslim state. Gandhi was deeply troubled by the idea of India being split in two. He tried to convince Jinnah that it was possible for Muslims and Hindus to live together as brothers, but his pleading was in vain. The negotiations between them failed, confrontations multiplied, and all over India men within the two communities began to kill each other. Thus, once again, Gandhi took up his bamboo walking stick and set out to "dry the tears of every eye" by preaching reconciliation. Despite the insults that were hurled at him and the broken bottles that some threw in his path, Gandhi did not give up.

The Blood of

India was on the brink of civil war when a new Viceroy, Lord Mountbatten, was appointed to end the British presence in India. He was well aware of the situation's gravity, but had very little time to act. Despite his and Gandhi's efforts to reason with Jinnah, as well as Nehru, who could no longer believe in a united India, the partition of India had become inevitable. Pakistan's borders were hastily drawn, cutting villages in two and separating families. As Muslims were the majority in Bengal (to the east) and Punjab (to the extreme west) the new country of Pakistan was made up of two regions over 1,000 miles apart!

Jinnah

On August 15, 1947, at 12:01 am, India became an independent country under Nehru's leadership, and Pakistan, the world's first Muslim country, was born. Gandhi, who was at the home of an untouchable, fell asleep deeply disheartened after praying for everyone's safety. India's partition led to one of the largest exoduses of all time. Nearly ten million people set out, with Hindus heading to India and Muslims to Pakistan. The two communities clashed in confrontations of unprecedented violence. "Today, India is a river of blood," wrote one American journalist.

Gandhi with Lord Moutbatten and his wife.

Liberty

LORD MOUNTBATTEN

Lord Mountbatten, who was a descendant of Queen Victoria and a cousin to the King of England, was 46 years old when he became the last Indian Viceroy. Gifted with an astonishing capacity for work and powerful decision-making abilities, Lord Mountbatten behaved quite differently from his predecessors. So much so that Nehru once said of him, *"Finally we have a real person for a Viceroy."* He not only tried to understand the Indians and their culture, but he also developed relationships of trust with the main Congress leaders. Gandhi was very fond of him and even went so far as to say that Lord Mountbatten *"echoes some of the values that burn in my own heart."* The two men shared a deep and genuine friendship.

The amphibious vehicle that carried Gandhi's ashes toward the water in Yamana. His ashes were cast into the middle of the river as thousands of orphans and others looked on.

In this climate of violence, Gandhi traveled to Calcutta, an enormous city teeming with beggars and lepers, where the risk of violence erupting was greater than anywhere else. With tensions between Hindus and Muslims running high, the city erupted into violence on August 31. Gandhi, almost 78, began a fast unto death, offering up his life in an effort to calm the madness that had gripped the country. By the second day of his fast, peaceful demonstrations began to appear, and murderers came weeping to the old man's bedside to lay down their still-bloody weapons. On September 4, 1947, civic leaders signed a communal declaration promising to combat all forces of religious hatred. Gandhi ended his hunger strike, having once again performed a miracle.

Several months later, on January 13, 1948, he again bent powerful leaders to his will by fasting, this time in Delhi. The Mahatma demanded the signing of a specifically worded charter that would guarantee the safety of all Muslims. Most important, he insisted that the Indian government pay the 550 million rupee debt that it owed to Pakistan. Five days later, as Gandhi lay dying, an agreement was signed. However, this time Hindu extremists thought that Gandhi had gone too far. They wanted the reunification of their country, and Gandhi had now become a traitor in their eyes. Having fasted for Muslims and played Pakistan's game, he had become an enemy that needed to be killed. A plot was hatched. The Hindu extremists had had enough.

The Martyr

On January 20, a failed assassination attempt was made. Ten days later, on January 30, 1948, as Gandhi walked to prayer assisted by his two grand nieces, he was approached by a man named Nathuram Godse. Pretending to bow, Godse drew a revolver from his sleeve and fired three shots at point-blank range. Gandhi collapsed immediately. It is widely thought that he called out to God as he fell. It was 5:30 pm on a winter's evening and the father of the nation was dead, shot by a Hindu.

India was in shock, and the world grieved. Heartbroken, Nehru was moved to compose his most beautiful speech, which he delivered as a radio address. *"The light has gone out of our lives"* he said, *"and there is darkness everywhere."* A national day of morning was proclaimed.

To the humble man whom England had so often humiliated, Lord Mountbatten gave a tribute worthy of the greatness that Gandhi had possessed. The Mahatma's body was covered in roses and carried in a funeral procession amidst a sea of people before it was cremated on a block of sandalwood. Twelve days later his ashes were scattered at the confluence of India's sacred rivers, the Ganges and the Yamuna. The man who possessed nothing was now gone, but he left behind him a universal message of love, tolerance, and non-violent struggle against injustice.

GANDHI'S ASSASSIN, A HINDU EXTREMIST

Nathuram Godse, born to a Brahmin family in 1910, was raised in strict accordance with Hindu tradition. He was a poor student, but instead of becoming a tailor as intended, he became passionate about politics at a very early age. He followed Gandhi for a while before joining Veer Savarkar, the fanatical prophet of militant Hinduism. He was a talented public speaker who didn't like crowds, and he liked women even less. In 1941 he met Apte, another Brahmin, who would become the mastermind behind the plot against Gandhi a few years later. During his trial, Godse claimed full responsibility for his crime and was condemned to death by hanging, as was his accomplice. He asked for his ashes to be saved until the day of India's reunification with Pakistan.

Being Hindu

What is Hinduism?

Hindusim is the religion practiced by the majority of India's inhabitants. With over 800 millions followers, it is one of the world's major religions. According to Hinduism the universe has always existed, and it follows an infinite cycle of birth, disappearance, and rebirth. Human beings follow this same pattern. They are born, they live and they die, after which they are reborn to another life. This is the cycle of reincarnation, or *samsara*. The quality of a person's life on earth is determined by *karma*, the record of good and bad deeds accumulated throughout past lives. In other words, one's actions determine one's future lives. For example, the least-deserving people can be reincarnated as the simplest animals. Hindus aspire to break free of this cycle and to achieve their final death, when they will at last dissolve into the cosmos. However, this final dissolution can only be attained through right action, true knowledge, and piety. Consequently, dedication to the most ancient Hindu scriptures, the *Vedas* (a collection of hymns, prayers, and ritual formulas that were formulated at least 1,500 years before Christ), is of vital importance.

A Pantheon of Gods

Hindus believe in many gods, some of which are more important than others. Interestingly, their names can change depending on place and circumstances, so the same god or goddess often has many different names. It also is true that some are specific to a particular village or even a particular family! Within the pantheon of gods, Vishnu and Shiva are highly honored. Vishnu, the god of stability, is responsible for maintaining the order of the world. He sometimes helps people by descending to earth as one of his incarnations, or *avatars* (*avatar* means "descent"). Shiva, the god of destruction and rejuvenation, creates and destroys. His wife Parvati is widely worshiped, along with many other goddesses. Most of these goddesses, however, are not worshiped independently, but only together with their husband.

DON'T GET CONFUSED!

Indians are the inhabitants of India. Hindus are people who practice Hinduism. Not all Indians are Hindus. Some Indians are Muslims, and others are Christians.

What Does it Mean to be Hindu?

Hinduism has no founder or organized church. It is highly tolerant of different forms of worship, and each Hindu can worship whatever god or gods he or she chooses. Normally, *puja*, the daily prayer, is observed twice a day, either at a temple or a family shrine. Whoever is leading the prayer (at temple it's a priest) stands before the statue of a god and presents offerings. These can be water, flowers, or the lighting of lamps. Ablutions (ritual baths where you purify yourself) are also very important in Hindu daily life. It is not possible to convert to Hinduism. To be a Hindu, you must be born a Hindu. Anyone is welcome to follow the teachings of a sage or guru, however.

Important Events

Millions of people gather together for the popular Hindu festivals. This strong communal spirit serves to bear witness to the continued strength of the Hindu faith. One such festival is *Holi*, which celebrates the arrival of spring. Nicknamed the Festival of Colors, it is celebrated by sprinkling oneself with water and colored powder. Then there is *Kumbh Mela*, which takes place every three years and is the oldest and most important Hindu festival. Thousands of pilgrims come at this time to bathe in the Ganges, a river so sacred that simply touching it cleanses one of all impurities.

Hindu pilgrims in Benares, India, around **1930.**.

"*So long as a man does not [...]
last among his fellow creatures[...]*

September 22, 1931, London. A throng of admirers try to get a closer look.

is own free will put himself
here is no salvation for him."

I claim to be a votary of truth from my child-hood. It was the most natural thing to me. My prayerful search gave me the revealing maxim "Truth is God" instead of the usual one, "God is Truth." That maxim enables me to see God face to face as it were. I feel him pervade every fiber of my being.

Gandhi, *Non-Violence in Peace and War, Volume 1*

Truth is my God. Non-violence is the means of realizing Him....

Gandhi, *Young India, May 6, 1926*

For we are all tarred with the same brush, and are children of one and the same Creator, and as such the divine powers within us are infinite. To slight a single human being is to slight those divine powers, and thus to harm not only that being but with him the whole world.

Gandhi, *Autobiography*

Truth is like a vast tree, which yields more and more fruit, the more you nurture it. The deeper the search in the mine of truth the richer the discovery of the gems buried there, in the shape of openings for an ever greater variety of service.

Gandhi, *Autobiography*

When the practice of *ahimsa* becomes universal, God will reign on earth as He does in heaven.

Gandhi, *Non-Violence in Peace and War, Volume 1*

I own that I have an unmovable faith in God and His goodness and unconsumable passion for truth and love. But is that not what every person has latent in him? If we are to make progress, we must not repeat history but make new history.... If we may make new discoveries and inventions in the phenomenal world, must we declare our bankruptcy in the spiritual domain?

Gandhi, *Young India*, May 6, 1926

It may be long before the law of love will be recognized in international affairs. The machineries of government stand between and hide the hearts of one people from those of another.

Gandhi, *Autobiography*

I swear by non-violence because I know that it alone conduces to the highest good of mankind, not merely in the next world, but in this also. I object to violence because, when it appears to do good, the good is only temporary, the evil it does is permanent....

Gandhi, *Young India, May 21, 1925*

The Way of

A non-violent revolution is not a program of seizure of power. It is a program of transformation of relationships, ending in a peaceful transfer of power.

Gandhi, *Non-Violence in Peace and War, Volume 2*

Non-violence is not a garment to be put on and off at will. Its seat is in the heart, and it must be an inseparable part of our very being.

Gandhi, *Non-Violence in Peace and War, Volume 1*

My optimism rests on my belief in the infinite possibilities of the individual to develop non-violence. The more you develop it in your own being, the more infectious it becomes till it overwhelms your surroundings and by and by might oversweep the world.

Gandhi, *Non-Violence in Peace and War, Volume 1*

Non-Violence

I claim to be a passionate seeker after truth, which is but another name for God. In the course of that search the discovery of non-violence came to me. Its spread is my life mission. I have no interest in living except for the prosecution of that mission.

Gandhi, *Non-Violence in Peace and War, Volume 1*

The first principle of non-violent action is that of non-cooperation with everything humiliating.

Gandhi, *Non-Violence in Peace and War, volume 1*

I hope to demonstrate that real Swaraj [Self-Rule] will come not by the acquisition of authority by a few but by the acquisition of the capacity by all to resist authority when abused. In other words, Swaraj is to be attained by educating the masses to a sense of their capacity to regulate and control authority.

Gandhi, *Young India, January 29, 1925*

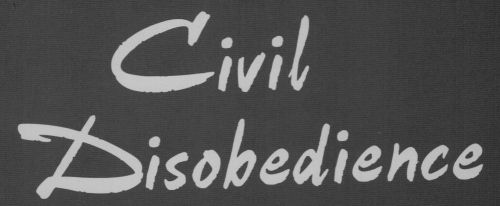

Civil Disobedience

The moment the slave resolves that he will no longer be a slave, his fetters fall. ...This may mean suffering. Your readiness to suffer will light the torch of freedom which can never be put out.

Gandhi, *Non-Violence in Peace and War, volume 2*

Mankind has to get out of violence only through non-violence. Hatred can be overcome only by love. Counter-hatred only increases the surface as well as the depth of hatred.

Gandhi, *Non-Violence in Peace and War, volume 2*

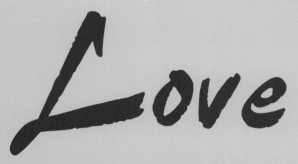

Love

Belief in non-violence is based on the assumption that human nature in its essence is one and therefore unfailingly responds to the advances of love....

Gandhi, *Harijan, December 24, 1938*

The greatest and most unimpeachable evidence of this force [Truth or Love] is to be found in the fact that, in spite of the wars of the world, it still lives on.

Thousands, indeed tens of thousands, depend for their existence on a very active working of this force. Little quarrels of millions of families in their daily lives disappear before the exercise of this force. Hundreds of nations live in peace. …Two brothers quarrel, one of them repents and reawakens the love…the two again live in peace….

Gandhi, *Autobiography*

Strength does not come from physical capacity.
It comes from an indomitable will.
A small body of determined spirits fired by an
unquenchable faith in their mission can alter
the course of history.
Gandhi

*The weak can never forgive. Forgiveness
is an attribute of the strong.* **Gandhi**

Strength

A weak-minded man can never be a *satyagrahi*. The
latter's "no" is invariably a "no" and his "yes" an
eternal "yes." Such a man has the strength to be a
devotee of truth and *ahimsa*. But here one must know
the difference between steadfastness and obstinacy.
If…one finds out that the decision was wrong and
in spite of that knowledge clings to it, that is
obstinacy and folly.

Gandhi, *Non-Violence in Peace and War, Volume 1*

I have not the shadow of a doubt that any man or woman can achieve what I have, if he or she would make the same effort and cultivate the same hope and faith. **Gandhi**

Goodness must be joined with knowledge. Mere goodness is not of much use, as I have found in life. One must cultivate the fine discriminating quality which goes with spiritual courage and character.

Gandhi, *Non-Violence in Peace and War, volume 2*

In the composition of the truly brave there should be no malice, no anger, no distrust, no fear of death or physical hurt.

Gandhi, *Non-Violence in Peace and War, Volume 1*

Courage

Mahatma Gandhi will go down in history on a par with Buddha and Jesus Christ.

Lord Mountbatten, the last British Viceroy of India

What has been said about

This is [Gandhi's] lesson and his legacy to the world: The evils we suffer cannot be eliminated by a violent attack in which one sector of humanity flies at another in destructive fury. Our evils are common and the solution of them can only be common. But we are not ready to undertake this common task because we are not ourselves. Consequently the first duty of every man is to return to his "right mind" in order that society itself may be sane. **Thomas Merton**

[Mahatma Gandh] was a man who made humility and simple truth more powerful than empires.
General George C. Marshall, *US Secretary of State*

If humanity is to progress, Gandhi is inescapable.... We may ignore him at our own risk."

Dr. Martin Luther King, Jr.

Gandhi

In India there came a man in our own generation who inspired us to great endeavor, ever reminding us that thought and action should never be divorced from moral principle, that the true path of man is the path of truth and peace.

Jawaharlal Nehru

Generations to come, it may be, will scarce believe that such a one as this, ever in flesh and blood, walked upon this earth.

Albert Einstein

Index

Ablutions, 51
Ahimsa, 7
  Gandhi on, 55
All-Indian Ambulance Corps, 35
Amritsar Massacre, 23, 37, 38
Apte, 48
Arjuna, 28
Avatars, 50

Bapu, defined, 40
Bhagavad Gita, 28, 32
Bible, 29
Boer War, 35
Boers, 31
Bombay (Mumbai), 26, 29, 36
Brahmacharya, 33
Brahmins, 26
Buddha, 63

Calcutta, 48
Caste system, 26, 45
Chauri Chaura, 39
Child marriage, 40
Churchill, Winston, 42
Civil disobedience, 23, 37, 40
  Gandhi on, 58
Coolie, defined, 13, 31
Courage, Gandhi on, 61

Delhi, 48
Dharasana salt factory, 42

Discipleship, Gandhi on, 6
Durban, 30, 31

Einstein, Albert, on Gandhi, 63
Equality, Gandhi on, 54, 55

Fasting, Gandhi on, 45
Festival of Colors, 51
Freedom, Gandhi on, 60

Gandhi, Laxmidas, 27
Gandhi, Manilal, 42
Gandhi, Mohandas
  advocacy of civil disobedience, 23, 37, 40
  advocacy of non-violence, 21, 23, 24-25, 34-35, 40
  and non-cooperation, 38-39, 58
  and untouchables, 45
  asceticism of, 32, 42
  ashram founded by, 19-20, 23, 32-33
  birth of activism of, 13-15, 30-31
  childhood character of, 26
  death of, 23, 48, 49
  family of, 26-27, 27, 32
  giving a speech, 10-11
  in London, 29, 52-53
  in South Africa, 15-18, 23, 28, 29-31, 34-35
  influence of Christ on, 34
  influence of Ruskin on, 32
  influence of Tolstoy on, 33
  life chronology of, 23

mission of, 42-43
on his mission, 6
pacifism of, 35, 46
parents of, 26-27
playing, 8
quotations about, 62-63
quotations and maxims of, 52-61
return to India, 36
return to London of, 42
wife of. *See* Kasturba

Ganges River, 49, 51
God, Gandhi on, 54, 55, 57
Godse, Nathuram, 23, 49
Goodness, Gandhi on, 61
Government, Gandhi on, 56
Great Epics, 28

Harishchandra, 26
Hinduism
    beliefs in, 50
    caste system in, 26, 45
    festivals of, 51
    holy books of, 28
    pantheon of, 50-51
    worship in, 51
Holi festival, 51

India
    British rule over, 36-37, 42-43
    independence of, 23
    partition of, 46-47
    racism in, 21-22, 36
    relations with Pakistan, 48
    religions of, 50
Indian National Congress, 32
    Gandhi and, 38
    origin of, 39

Irwin, Lord, 42
Jesus Christ, 29, 63
    influence on Gandhi, 34
Jinnah, Muhammad Ali, 46

Karma, 50
Kasturba, 23, 29, 30, 32
    character of, 20, 45
    death of, 46
King, Martin Luther, Jr., 32, 35
    on Gandhi, 63
The Kingdom of God Is Within You
    (Tolstoy), 33
Knowledge, Gandhi on, 61
Koran, 29
Krishna, 28
Kshatriyas, 26
Kumbh Mela, 51

Lancashire, 43
London, 29
    Gandhi's return to, 42
London Agreement, 45
Love, Gandhi on, 56, 59

Mahabharata, 28
Mahatma
    Gandhi given name of, 36
    meaning of term, 7
Maritzburg, 30
Marshall, George C., 62
Merton, Thomas, on Gandhi, 62
Morality, Gandhi on, 6
Mountbatten, Lord, 23, 46, 47, 47, 49
    on Gandhi, 62
Mumbai (Bombay), 26, 29, 36
Muslims, 40, 48

independent nation of, 46-47
Nehru, Jawaharlal, 41, 41, 43, 46-47, 49
  on Gandhi, 63
New Testament, 29
Non-cooperation, 38-39
  Gandhi on, 58
Non-violence, 21, 23, 40
  Gandhi on, 56-57, 59
  justification for, 24-25
  and prison, 35
  satyagraha, 34

Pacifism, 35, 46
Pakistan, birth of, 23, 47
Parvati, 50
Porbandar, 26, 36
Power, Gandhi on, 56
Pretoria, 30
Prison, as weapon of non-violence, 35
Puja, 51

Quit India campaign, 46

Racism
  in India, 21-22, 36
  in South Africa, 15-18, 30
Reincarnation, 50
Rowlatt Act, 37
Ruskin, John, 32

Sabarmati River, 36
Salt March, 23
Salt tax, 40, 42
Samsara, 50
Satyagraha, 34-35

BIBLIOGRAPHY   *(All quotes come from these books and the websites below.)*

Gandhi, Mohandas Karamchand. *Autobiography, The Story of My Experiments with Truth*. Illinois: BN Publishing, 2008.

Merton, Thomas, ed. *Gandhi on Non-Violence*. New York: New Directions, 2007.

Fischer, Louis, ed. *The Essential Gandhi, An Anthology of His Writings on His Life, Work, and Ideas*. New York: Vintage Books, 2002.

FURTHER READING

Fischer, Louis. *Gandhi: His Life and Message for the World*. New York: New American Library, Signet Books, 1954.

Fischer, Louis. *The Life of Mahatma Gandhi*. New York: Macmillan, Collier Books, 1962.

O'Brien, Anne Sibley and Perry Edmond O'Brien. *After Gandhi, One Hundred Years of Nonviolent Resistance*. Massachusetts: Charlesbridge, 2009.

Pastan, Amy. *Gandhi, A Photographic Story of A Life*. New York: DK Publishing, 2006.

Severance, John B. *Gandhi: Great Soul*. New York: Clarion Books, 1997.

Wilkinson, Philip. *Gandhi: The Young Protestor Who Founded a Nation*. Washington, D.C.: National Geographic, 2005.

Visit www.mkgandhi.org to read more about Gandhi's life, work and ideas. This site is run by Gandhi Organizations in India.

Visit www.mahatma.com to read Gandhi's own words and to find out more about his legacy.

Picture Research
Nicole Bouchereau

Picture Credits
FIA / Rue des Archives: p. 24-25.
Gamma: p. 27, p. 32, p. 39.
Hulton archive / Getty Images: p. 52-53.
Keystone France: p. 4-5, p. 8, p. 38 (Mary Evans), p. 41, p. 43, p. 48, p. 51.
Roger-Violet: p. 37.
Rue des Archives: p. 28.
Rue des Archives / SVB: p. 10-11.
Rue des Archives / PVDE: p. 47.